Legacy
Builders
_of_ Antiquity

UNVEILING THE SECRETS OF TIMELESS PARABLES
IN BUSINESS DEVELOPMENT

SAMSON SAMUEL

ISBN: 9798871088982

First Edition: December 2023

www.samsonbiz.com

Dedication

The book that I have authored holds a significant place in my heart. I take this opportunity to dedicate it to all the gentle readers.

I dedicate this book to my beloved and cherished wife, Jelia, who has been my partner throughout the ups and downs of my journey. She has stood by my side, supported me, and prayed for me every step of the way. I am truly blessed to have her in my life and grateful for her unwavering love and support.

I also dedicate this book to my son, Zane, who has inspired me to continue this life journey. He is an invaluable treasure that God has bestowed upon me, and I am grateful for his love and encouragement every day.

I express my heartfelt gratitude to Jelia and Zane for being my constant inspiration and motivation in my endeavors. After Him, you are the greatest treasures God has given me!

Acknowledgments

I cannot express enough gratitude for the invaluable support and guidance I received from my mentor and accomplished author, Sweta Samota, at the beginning of my journey as an author. With her phenomenal expertise and motivation, I completed my book and succeeded today.

I am also profoundly grateful to Joseph Mathew for his unwavering belief in my abilities and for providing encouragement and support that helped me overcome challenges throughout the writing process. His faith in my work has been a source of inspiration and a driving force behind my success.

I owe a debt of gratitude to Shane D'Souza, Telivus Media Private Limited, India, who played an instrumental role in developing my book. His ingenious and insightful suggestions, constructive criticism, and valuable advice were crucial in shaping my work and bringing it to fruition.

I would also like to extend my most profound appreciation to Clint Estibeiro, Sky Staffing Solutions, Ireland, for his unwavering guidance and practical suggestions. His help was invaluable in navigating the challenges of the writing process and bringing my vision to life.

Finally, I would like to express my heartfelt thanks to my dear friends and supporters, Bryan Pereira and family, Charles Goes and family, Jackson Darwin and family, and Zanen Jacob and family, who never let me down and provided me with unwavering support and assistance throughout my journey. I am genuinely grateful for their encouragement and belief in my work.

Contents

Introduction

A chieving success in today's world, with its perpetual changes and intense competition, has become an ongoing pursuit that requires solving a complex puzzle. As we navigate the intricate business development landscape, we often need guidance, a beacon of light to illuminate our path toward success. Despite being smaller than many major cities, Israel has emerged as a global leader in entrepreneurship and innovation, and its success can be attributed to ancient parables that have been passed down through the ages.

The scrolls containing these parables, found in the Gospels of Matthew and Luke, have captivated readers for centuries, they offer moral and ethical lessons that resonate with people from all walks of life. These parables have profoundly impacted the character and behavior of the Israelites, shaping their innovation and entrepreneurship. They have provided a powerful blueprint that has unlocked the potential of the nation to become a leader in commerce, entrepreneurship, and innovation.

This study examines nine remarkable parables that reflect the nature of business development and demonstrate how Israel has used their wisdom to achieve noteworthy success in the global marketplace. These parables contain universal truths, offering valuable insights into strategy, ethics, leadership, and resilience, which are the cornerstones of Israel's remarkable journey as an economic power.

The ancient parables are simple narratives communicating profound ideas, making them accessible and impactful. Through their application, Israel has become a true leader in business development, earning a reputation for its remarkable ability to turn adversity into opportunity. The timeless wisdom in these parables has guided Israel's incredible journey as an economic power.

The Israeli people's ingenuity, adaptability, and unwavering determination have enabled them to thrive in a rapidly changing world while remaining true to the timeless wisdom in the ancient parables. This study guides modern entrepreneurs, leaders, and visionaries worldwide, empowering them to tap into the timeless knowledge that can transform their approach to daily life, business development, and innovation. It reveals how Israel has harnessed the power of these universal truths to achieve remarkable success in the global marketplace, providing valuable lessons for all who seek to follow in their footsteps.

"Every work is a business,

and every businessperson is a diligent worker,

*for **SUCCESS** is built upon the foundation*

of unwavering dedication and hard labor."

Samson Samuel

Foundations Of Success

"A wise man who built his house on the rock.

The rain came down, the streams rose,

and the winds blew

and beat against that house; yet it did not fall,

because it had its foundation on the rock.

A foolish man who built his house on sand.

The rain came down, the streams rose,

> *and the winds blew and beat against that house,*
>
> *and it fell with a great crash."*

Parable of the Two Builders
Mathew 7:24-27

The parable of the wise man who built his house on a rock and the foolish man who built his house on sand is a powerful fable that resonates with individuals seeking to excel in business development. This allegory provides profound insights that directly apply to successful entrepreneurship principles. It perfectly illustrates the essence of enterprise development, which involves achieving lasting success through careful strategic planning, resilience, and a foundation built on solid principles.

The story represents the obstacles, challenges, and uncertainties businesses will inevitably face and how they can be overcome. The rain, streams, and winds symbolize the fierce competition, changing market conditions, and other external factors threatening a business's survival. The decisions made during the startup phase are critical since they determine whether a business will stand firm like a house on the rock or crumble under pressure like a house on the sand. Therefore, a strong foundation built on a solid business plan, a clear vision, and a commitment to excellence is vital for enduring success. This timeless parable reminds us that intelligent planning, resilience, and a solid foundation are the keys to success in business.

The Strategic Foundation: Crafting a Resilient Vision

Developing a business successfully necessitates a well-crafted strategic vision that is the cornerstone of an entrepreneur's plan and guides all decisions and actions. A strategic vision is essential in establishing a solid foundation in the marketplace, just as a wise man recognizes the importance of a solid foundation. A well-defined strategic vision includes a deep understanding of the industry, target audience, competitive landscape, and a clear vision for growth. It sets the direction, defines the purpose, and fuels the passion for the business, ensuring that every decision, investment, and effort is aligned with long-term goals.

A comprehensive strategic vision should encompass a detailed analysis of the industry, including market trends, consumer behavior, and potential growth opportunities. Target audience research should also be integral to the strategic vision, providing insights into the target customer's needs, preferences, and behaviors. By identifying the competition and their strengths and weaknesses, entrepreneurs can develop strategies to differentiate their business and gain a competitive edge.

A well-structured strategic foundation is essential to withstand the challenges of a dynamic marketplace. It provides resilience, enabling businesses to remain agile and adapt to changing trends and consumer behavior. A business can withstand the storms of uncertainty and change by creating a resilient framework.

As a visionary leader, it is essential to know where the business wants to go and ensure that every decision is aligned with that strategic goal. A comprehensive strategic vision provides the necessary framework to achieve long-term success, guiding all decisions and actions, ensuring the business remains focused on its goals, and enabling it to thrive in a dynamic marketplace.

Market Research: Understanding the Terrain

Building a successful business is a complex process requiring a solid infrastructure, and knowledge is the cornerstone. The parable of the wise man emphasizes the importance of a meticulous examination of the landscape before constructing a business on a solid base. Similarly, building a business with a well-thought-out strategy is similar to building on a rock. It is essential to undertake comprehensive market research to understand your business's target audience, competitors, industry trends, and potential risks.

A sound strategy comprises market analysis, competitive intelligence, a forward-looking approach rooted in careful market research, exhaustive analysis, and an integrated business expansion approach. To develop a successful strategy, it is crucial to keep yourself updated with the latest industry trends and continuously learn. With this knowledge, you will be better equipped to respond to market changes with necessary adjustments and innovations, ensuring your business remains stable, even in turbulent market conditions.

Market research is a vital component of the strategy, as it helps you gain insights into the market, including customer preferences, market size, competition, pricing, and distribution channels. A strategy that needs more solid market research and analysis is based on unfounded assumptions, making it vulnerable to sudden changes. Therefore, a comprehensive market analysis is necessary to identify opportunities, threats, strengths, and weaknesses. With the correct data, you can develop a strategy tailored to your business's unique needs, goals, and objectives.

Competitive intelligence is another crucial element of a successful business strategy. It involves gathering information about your competitors, including their strengths, weaknesses, market share, pricing, and marketing strategies. By analyzing your competitors, you can identify gaps in the market, potential partnerships, and areas for improvement. This information can help you develop a competitive advantage and differentiate your business.

Developing a sound business strategy requires thorough market research, competitive intelligence, and a forward-looking approach. It's essential to continuously learn and stay updated on industry trends to strengthen your business. Creating a flexible framework that can adapt to the ever-changing business landscape is crucial to weathering uncertain times and securing long-term success for your business.

Building a Skilled Team: Constructing Walls

In the business development world, any enterprise's success depends mainly on the strength and resilience of the team. A team functions as the foundation of a structure, built brick by brick. Therefore, selecting the right team members with the proper skills, experience, and passion for the industry is critical. Hiring people who share vision and values creates a solid foundation that can withstand challenges and sustain growth despite adversity.

A critical factor in building a successful team is identifying and recruiting individuals with specialized skills that complement each other. This ensures that the business is not reliant on one person and can adapt to changing market conditions. The team members should possess individual talents and the ability to collaborate effectively, communicate openly, and work in unison toward a common goal. This cohesion is essential to tackling complex projects, managing conflict, and ensuring everyone is headed in the same direction.

In business, challenges and uncertainties are inevitable. However, a team with the right skills is better equipped to face market adversity, reorient itself, when necessary, develop innovative solutions, and remain resilient even when market conditions deteriorate. Invest in ongoing training and development to keep your team ahead of the curve in a rapidly evolving business world. Encourage open and transparent communication between team members. Effective communication is vital to welding a team together and fostering a culture of collaboration, growth, and resilience.

An experienced team knows the importance of analyzing failures, finding the root causes, making changes to avoid repetition, innovating, and staying ahead of the competition. Cultivate a continuous learning and development culture to build a solid, consistent team to weather any storm. Building a strong team is not a one-time affair but an ongoing process that requires dedication, commitment, and a willingness to adapt to change. With the right team, a business can achieve its goals, overcome challenges, and thrive in today's competitive market.

Financial Prudence: Strengthening the Roof

As a homeowner, you know that a solid and durable roof is critical to protect your home from the elements. Similarly, in the business world, financial prudence is equally essential to safeguard the long-term success of your enterprise. To ensure the economic viability of your operation, it is necessary to prioritize financial intelligence. This involves developing a comprehensive understanding of financial statements, cash flow management, and taxation to make informed decisions.

Creating a detailed budget that includes all expenses, revenue projections, and contingency reserves is necessary to establish a solid financial foundation. Developing a long-term financial plan for your business and diversifying revenue sources to minimize risk exposure is also essential. Conducting regular expense analyses can help you identify areas where cost reductions or optimizations can be made to ensure financial stability. Additionally, maintaining healthy cash flow, controlling expenses, and minimizing debt are crucial to your business's ability to withstand economic downturns.

Reinvesting profits, planning for growth, and building reserves are all critical factors in making informed financial decisions that can ensure the longevity of your business. Emergency funds or reserves can help you weather difficult times without compromising your business's stability. Consider risk management strategies such as insurance, contracts, and legal protections to safeguard your enterprise. This includes planning for savings, investments, and retirement for your business and its employees.

Employing sound financial management practices, efficient budgeting, and strategic investments can help you protect your operations, create opportunities to invest in growth initiatives, and ensure your business remains adaptable during economic downturns. This will enable you to capitalize on strategic opportunities, expand your market reach, and innovate without risking financial instability. By cultivating skilled teams and practicing financial prudence, your business can ensure its long-term success and resilience in facing challenges. Ultimately, this will enable your business to weather any storm that comes its way and secure a prosperous future.

Adaptability: Withstanding the Storms

The parable highlights the importance of adaptability in contrast to rigidness, portraying the significance of flexibility and change. The rainfall, rising currents, and strong winds depicted in the parable symbolize market fluctuations, competitive pressures, and technological advancements, respectively, that businesses must face and adapt to. Adapting to market conditions and consumer preferences changes in business development is paramount as it allows a business to remain relevant and competitive.

Adapting to the ever-changing business landscape is crucial to ensure a business's survival and success. The ability to innovate, reorient, and take flexible positions is critical to overcoming even the toughest challenges. Businesses must diversify their product or service offerings and keep up with emerging trends to stay ahead of the curve. Innovation is the driving force that propels businesses forward by developing new ways and methods to keep their business relevant and resilient.

A business founded on strategic foresight and adaptability can endure even the most strenuous challenges. Such a business values steady growth, ethical practices, and responsible decision-making, ensuring the business thrives for future generations. Developing a value proposition that caters to the customers' needs is vital to achieving this. This foundation sets the business apart from its competitors, giving customers a compelling reason to choose it over others. Adapting is the key to long-term success in a world of constant change.

Customer-Centric Approach: Building Relationships

Building and maintaining relationships is a critical part of running a successful business. It is essential to have a customer-centric approach, where the focus is on understanding and addressing your customers' needs. This involves providing high-quality products or services and actively engaging with your customers to build a strong relationship with them.

Building strategic partnerships, nurturing customer relationships, and creating a collaborative work environment are essential to establishing a solid foundation. This means taking the time to understand your customers' requirements, providing them with value, and creating loyalty. It is also necessary to prioritize customer service, actively listen to feedback, and continuously deliver value.

Building solid customer relationships can create advocates promoting your products or services to others. This not only helps to create a loyal customer base but also helps your business withstand external pressures.

In addition, forming strategic partnerships with other businesses, suppliers, and stakeholders can be beneficial. This approach provides stability during uncertain times and opens up new avenues for growth. By consistently providing value and solving problems, your business can survive even the most challenging conditions.

Overall, establishing and maintaining relationships is crucial for building a successful business. This requires a customer-centric approach, prioritizing customer service, and forming strategic partnerships to create a solid foundation to withstand external pressures.

Learning from Failure: Lessons from the House on Sand

In the contemporary business world, the adoption of an agile mindset is not only beneficial but also imperative for success. The Foolish Man's House on Sand illustrates the significance of learning from mistakes and the danger of overlooking a solid foundation. In the field of business development, setbacks and failures can provide valuable insights and serve as powerful lessons. Building on sand is a hasty and shortsighted decision, just as prioritizing short-term profits requires comprehensive research to avoid long-term instability. As a result, a wise business developer recognizes the importance of analyzing setbacks and identifying weaknesses to reinforce the foundation and prevent future crashes.

The learning process in business development is akin to rebuilding on a firmer foundation, which promotes continuous improvement and lasting success. Failures should be viewed as opportunities for growth, learning, and improvement. By analyzing failures, you can refine your business strategies and ensure that history does not repeat itself. The ability to respond quickly to market changes, learn from failures, and integrate new insights is vital to a successful strategy. Therefore, a sound business development strategy should consider short-term gains and long-term sustainability.

We must delve into concrete, real-life examples to illustrate the point. Let's take a moment to reflect on their actions.

Tata Group

The Tata Group is a conglomerate with a long and storied history from 1868. Founded by Jamsetji Tata, it has grown into a global enterprise with a presence in various industries, including steel, automobiles, information technology, and more. The Tata Group's success can be attributed to its commitment to core values and principles, such as integrity, social responsibility, and ethical business practices. These principles have guided the group's expansion and adaptation to changing markets and technologies.

Infosys

Infosys is one of India's leading information technology services businesses. Founded in 1981 by Narayana Murthy and a group of co-founders, Infosys has become a global player in IT services. It has achieved lasting success through its focus on innovation, employee-centric practices, and a commitment to delivering high-quality client services. Infosys's ability to adapt to changing technology landscapes, strategic planning, and emphasis on corporate governance and ethics have been critical factors in its enduring success.

The parable of the wise man who built his house on a rock reminds the realm of business development that a strong foundation is crucial for sustainable growth. To overcome and thrive amidst the challenges of the ever-changing market landscape, it is imperative to develop a clear vision, conduct thorough research, build a competent team, manage finances prudently, and remain adaptable. It's a metaphor and a practical approach to business development success.

Therefore, entrepreneurs and business developers should learn from the wisdom of the ages, as the rock represents the foundation of their success. By adhering to the sage's wisdom, businesses can endure uncertainties and emerge more robust, resilient, and firmly established in their strategic vision. In conclusion, a solid foundation is not only necessary but also critical for sustainable growth and success in the field of business development.

The Mighty Potential Within

"A mustard seed, which a man took

and planted in his field.

Though it is the smallest of all seeds, when it grows,

it is the largest of garden plants and becomes a tree,

so that the birds come and perch in its branches."

Parable of the Mustard Seed
Mathew 13:31-32

The parable of the mustard seed is an inspiring and thought-provoking story that teaches a valuable lesson about the potential for exponential growth, even from the smallest beginnings. According to the parable, a man plants a tiny mustard seed in his field, which may initially seem insignificant. Eventually, he grows into the most significant garden plant, providing shelter and food for those around it. This story highlights the importance of nurturing small beginnings, which can lead to substantial growth and prosperity.

In business development, the parable of the mustard seed is an apt metaphor for the journey of entrepreneurship. Like the mustard seed, a small business can grow into a giant in its industry with the right strategy, commitment, and promotion. However, it all starts with a small beginning, and the key is to focus on fostering that beginning into a sustainable and thriving business.

The lesson from the parable of the mustard seed is clear: do not underestimate the power of small beginnings. In today's world, where startups are becoming increasingly popular, and entrepreneurship is rising, this story serves as a reminder that even the smallest of businesses can achieve great success with the right approach. By nurturing small beginnings, entrepreneurs can create thriving businesses that attract customers, partners, and investors.

Seed Selection: Identifying Opportunities

Starting a business is like planting a mustard seed. Just as a farmer selects the finest seeds to ensure a successful harvest, an entrepreneur must choose the right business idea, concept, or product to develop. It is essential to remember that even though the initial idea may be small and unassuming, it has the potential for significant growth. Therefore, it is crucial to invest time and resources in refining the concept and making it unique and valuable.

Extensive research and analysis are necessary to ensure the business idea caters to the market's requirements. Entrepreneur should look for opportunities that align with their expertise and passion and have the potential for substantial growth. A well-chosen "seed" can be the foundation of a future business tree.

Developing a roadmap for the business is vital to establish achievable milestones. This roadmap should include a comprehensive plan for the business, including marketing strategies, a budget, and a timeline for reaching specific goals. The entrepreneur should remain flexible and open to adjustments as the business grows and evolves.

Remember, starting a business is a journey that requires patience, hard work, and dedication. The mustard seed is a reminder that even the most modest beginnings can lead to significant outcomes. With careful planning, commitment, and perseverance, any business can thrive.

Planting: Launching Your Venture

Starting a business is comparable to planting a seed. Before embarking on this journey, it is crucial to identify a viable business idea, much like selecting the right seed for the soil. This process requires much research and analysis to determine the market's needs and the competition's strengths and weaknesses.

Once the right business idea has been identified, the next step is to dedicate time and energy to the initial investment and effort required to establish the business. This process is like sowing the "mustard seed," which necessitates fertile soil and consistent nurturing to ensure growth and development.

A business owner or leader must have a clear vision and ambitious goals, regardless of how small or significant they may seem. It is also essential to select the market and niche wisely and possess in-depth knowledge of the target audience's needs and preferences. Establishing a compelling brand identity and reaching the intended audience effectively requires a robust business plan, securing funding, and developing a sturdy structure.

To ensure long-term success, it is vital to create high-quality products that cater to the customers' needs and streamline procedures to optimize productivity while minimizing waste. Although the returns on this investment may take time, it is indispensable for long-term success. Like planting a mustard seed, a business requires a solid foundation to flourish and grow into a successful venture.

Nurturing Growth: Building a Strong Base

Throughout history, the mustard seed has been used as an allegory for big things coming in small packages. It's considered the smallest of all seeds yet holds tremendous potential for growth. This analogy is particularly fitting for effective business development, which involves investing time, money, and resources into promoting and expanding a business through various means such as marketing, research, or product development.

Just like a mustard seed, a business requires the right conditions to thrive, and this is achieved through the implementation of a robust development strategy that revolves around creating a solid organizational structure, investing in employees, and providing excellent products or services. It's not just about getting off to a good start; it's about laying the foundation for sustainable growth.

A successful business development strategy prioritizes growth, commitment to creating value for customers, employees, and the community, and offering exceptional customer service to build loyalty and generate word-of-mouth referrals. Maintaining a healthy financial structure and reinvesting profits for growth are essential. However, a thriving business should aspire to have a positive impact beyond profits.

The strategy should focus on developing solid roots by building a robust infrastructure, creating a unique value proposition, and laying the foundation for sustainable growth. This includes investing in the right people, developing a solid culture, and fostering an environment of learning and continuous improvement. Change should be embraced as a catalyst for growth, and consistent nurturing is essential for scaling up.

Despite its small size, a mustard seed possesses immense growth potential. Any business can thrive and achieve sustainable success by implementing a well-thought-out business development strategy that prioritizes growth, values people, and embraces change.

Branching Out: Expanding Horizons

The transformation of a tiny mustard seed into a tall and sturdy tree is a timeless symbol of growth, expansion, and potential. Similarly, in the business world, identifying opportunities for scaling up, branching out, and diversifying is crucial for sustained success and growth. To achieve this, businesses must leverage their core strengths, constantly improve their operations, and remain flexible and adaptable in changing market conditions and customer needs.

One of the most effective ways to explore new avenues of growth and expansion is through strategic partnerships, joint ventures, and collaborations with other businesses or industry players. This can help businesses tap into new markets, access new customers, and leverage complementary resources and expertise. Additionally, introducing new product lines, services, or features can help businesses broaden their portfolio and appeal to a broader range of customers. Expanding their operations to recent geographic locations can help them tap into new markets and customer segments.

As businesses grow and evolve, they may need to hire more employees, invest in new technologies or equipment, or diversify their offerings to stay competitive and meet the changing needs of their customers. This requires a strong focus on operational excellence, continuous improvement, customer-centricity, and a willingness to embrace change and innovation.

In today's fast-paced and ever-changing business landscape, the key to success lies in being agile, adaptable, and customer-focused. By capitalizing on its strengths, exploring new opportunities, and consistently improving its operations, a business can establish a solid and sustainable foundation for growth and profitability. This allows the business to stay ahead of the curve while delivering value to its customers.

Sustainability: Ensuring Long-Term Success

Developing and maintaining a successful enterprise is a challenging endeavor that requires a long-term vision and a commitment to sustainability. It is crucial to recognize that businesses evolve like a mustard seed that blossoms into a large tree. However, instead of rushing into hasty decisions or reckless expansions, it is essential to exercise patience and perseverance while investing in systems, processes, and skilled employees to support growth while maintaining quality.

In addition to investing in the appropriate resources, businesses should prioritize ethical and environmentally responsible measures. This includes collaborating with complementary organizations to achieve mutually beneficial goals, enhancing the customer experience, and continuously developing innovative products or services. This approach allows businesses to stay ahead of the competition while remaining adaptable and resilient to market changes and challenges.

It is important to remember that the size of a business only sometimes determines its success. Instead, the quality of its products or services and the value it provides to its customers are crucial factors that contribute to long-term growth and sustainability. Therefore, businesses should focus on creating customer value while prioritizing sustainable practices.

Ultimately, the journey to success requires dedication, hard work, and a willingness to adapt and innovate. By prioritizing sustainability and investing in the appropriate resources, businesses can steadily grow and achieve sustainable results that benefit both the organization and its stakeholders.

Attracting Stakeholders and Customers: Creating a Thriving Ecosystem

Your business must take a page from the mustard tree's book to attract potential opportunities and partnerships. The mustard tree provides a nurturing environment for birds, much like your organization should provide a nurturing environment for stakeholders, including investors, partners, and customers. This can be achieved by establishing a solid and reputable brand image, delivering unparalleled value, and demonstrating an unwavering commitment to excellence.

To ensure that stakeholders perceive significant value in your business, it is essential to cultivate robust relationships within your industry and local community. This can be done by sharing your expertise and becoming a trusted resource. Doing so can establish a thriving network and community around your brand.

In addition, cultivating meaningful connections with seasoned professionals can offer guidance and unlock new opportunities. These connections can provide invaluable resources, mentors, and support to drive your business's growth and transform it into a collaboration, investment, and expansion hub.

By fostering relationships, delivering exceptional value, and creating a flourishing ecosystem around your business, you can establish a strong foundation for sustainable success. Remember that building a successful business is not just about what you know but also about who you know and the relationships you make.

Reaping the Harvest: Enjoying the Fruits of Success

Running a successful business requires a meticulous strategy, undivided dedication, and ample patience. The journey toward success is a long and winding road, and it is essential to have perseverance and unwavering commitment to keep moving forward. The story of the mustard seed is a perfect example of how even the most minor ventures can achieve remarkable growth with a well-structured business development strategy and a solid commitment to its growth.

It is crucial to recognize your business's potential and remember that it all starts with a seed - your vision and determination. Entrepreneurs must be willing to take risks and invest their time and resources into nurturing their ventures. With the right market, dedicated efforts, and continuous adjustments, one can transform a small idea into a thriving enterprise that reaches new heights.

Small businesses are the backbone of any economy, and it is essential to acknowledge their potential. They catalyze growth by creating jobs and contributing to the economy. However, success is not a one-time event but a journey that requires continuous effort and adjustment. Embracing these principles and maintaining a steadfast approach can help a business grow and thrive beyond one's wildest expectations.

Let's examine some real-life actions as current examples.

Patanjali Ayurved

Patanjali Ayurved, founded by Baba Ramdev and Acharya Balkrishna in 2006, is a prime example of a small business that rapidly grew into a significant player in the Indian consumer goods and FMCG (Fast-Moving Consumer Goods) industry. The business primarily produces and markets Ayurvedic and herbal products, including healthcare, personal care, and food products. Patanjali's success can be attributed to its commitment to promoting natural and traditional Indian products, an aggressive marketing strategy, and the increasing demand for healthier and more natural consumer goods.

Zomato

Zomato, founded by Deepinder Goyal and Pankaj Chaddah in 2008, started as a small restaurant discovery and food delivery platform in India. Through strategic expansion, commitment to customer satisfaction, and innovative marketing, Zomato has transformed into a global giant in online food delivery and restaurant discovery. The business's growth story is a testament to its ability to adapt to changing consumer preferences, expand into international markets, and maintain a solid online presence through effective promotion and branding.

In conclusion, the success of a business is not an overnight achievement but a result of a well-crafted strategy, dedicated efforts, and continuous adjustments. Entrepreneurs must have the courage to take risks, believe in their vision, and invest in the growth of their venture. With perseverance and a steadfast approach, even the most miniature ideas can become thriving enterprises that generate substantial returns, promote prosperity, and create opportunities for all associated.

Sow to Grow

"*A farmer went out to sow his seed.*

As he was scattering the seed, some fell along the

path, and the birds came and ate it up.

Some fell on rocky places,

where they did not have much soil.

It sprang up quickly, because the soil was shallow.

But when the sun came up, the plants were scorched,

and they withered because they had no root.

Other seeds fell among thorns,

which grew up and choked the plants.

Still other seeds fell on good soil,

where it produced a crop —

a hundred, sixty, or thirty times what was sown."

Parable of the Sower
Mathew 13:3-8

The Parable of the Sower, alternatively known as the parable of the farmer who sows the seed, is a famous allegory used to depict the dissemination of ideas, beliefs, or knowledge among receptive "soils" in people's minds. The parable is a valuable and insightful tool to comprehend businesses' different environments or niches and how those environments can impact their growth and success. It is an engaging representation of the concept of "niche" in business development that offers valuable lessons for individuals and businesses seeking to succeed in today's competitive business environment.

In business development, a niche refers to a specialized segment or market within a more significant industry or market. It is a unique and distinct area where a business can focus its products, services, and marketing efforts to meet a particular customer's needs and preferences. Establishing a niche requires thoroughly understanding the customer's needs, preferences, behavior, competencies, values, and objectives.

Like the farmer who sows his seeds in different soils, individuals and businesses strive to establish themselves in niches that match their competencies, values, and objectives. The Parable of the Sower offers valuable insight into the different types of soil that represent various business environments. The seeds, conversely, symbolize a business idea, product, or even individuals seeking acceptance and growth in a particular area.

The parable has four types of soil: the path, rocky ground, thorns, and good soil. The path represents people who need help understanding or care about the idea or product being presented to them. The rocky ground represents people who are receptive to the concept but need more depth to sustain it. The thorns represent people who are receptive to the idea but are too preoccupied with other things to pursue it. The good soil represents people who are receptive to the idea and are willing to invest time, effort, and resources to nurture it.

By understanding the different environments and niches, businesses can strategically position themselves to maximize their chances of success. They can focus on creating a product or service that meets the needs and preferences of a particular group of customers and tailor their marketing efforts to reach those customers effectively. The Parable of the Sower is a helpful allegory that offers valuable lessons for individuals and businesses seeking to succeed in today's competitive business environment.

Scattering Seeds Along the Path (Unfocused Approach)

Have you ever tried to introduce a new idea or offer to someone who needs to be more receptive or attentive? It can be a difficult and frustrating experience. It's like scattering seeds along a path and hoping they will grow. Similarly, taking a broad, non-targeted approach in business can lead to similar results. When you must clearly understand your target audience, your business idea or product may be quickly dismissed or unappreciated, making it vulnerable to market forces and competitors.

This is especially true in niche markets. You may struggle to gain traction if you don't identify your audience, even if you have a great idea or product. The problem is that niche markets are already saturated with competitors, and people are often not actively seeking new ideas or products. As a result, capturing potential customers' attention can be challenging, and you may need help to build a customer base.

To succeed in a niche market, you must identify an audience actively seeking or open to the niche you want to address. This requires a targeted approach that focuses on the needs and preferences of the identified audience. Doing so can increase the chances of success for your business idea or product.

It's also important to note that a targeted approach can mean something other than limiting your audience. Instead, it means understanding your audience and developing a strategy that resonates with them. This can involve identifying sub-niches within your niche market and tailoring your approach to each group. Doing so can maximize your potential customer base and increase your chances of success.

Introducing new ideas or products requires a clear understanding of your target audience. Developing a targeted approach tailored to your audience's needs and preferences can increase your chances of success in a niche market. So, take the time to identify your audience and develop a strategy that resonates with them. It may take some extra effort, but the payoff can be significant.

Falling on Rocky Places (Shallow Engagement)

In business, the phrase "rocky ground" is commonly used to describe an environment that may appear promising initially but lacks the depth and substance necessary for sustained success. It's like a seedling that sprouts quickly in shallow soil, indicating a niche where there may be initial interest but a need for proper understanding, commitment, and connection. This often leads to a sudden retreat when faced with challenges. Entrepreneurs who venture into these niches may experience rapid growth. Still, with a solid business plan and infrastructure, they can handle setbacks and will likely continue their efforts when faced with difficulties or competing priorities. When the challenges or competition increase, businesses, like plants with shallow roots, will struggle to survive and eventually wither away. Therefore, entrepreneurs need initial enthusiasm and a comprehensive understanding of the market, a solid business plan, and the necessary infrastructure to support their venture in the long run.

Falling Among Thorns (Market Saturation)

The symbolic representation of a seed amidst thorns in business signifies the challenges a new idea or offering may face while trying to establish itself in a highly competitive, saturated market. The "thorns" refer to the hindrances, diversions, and competing priorities that can impede the growth of a business. In such situations, it can be challenging to succeed and establish a unique identity, mainly if you belong to a niche market with numerous similar businesses.

For instance, if you are trying to enter a market already dominated by established players, you may need help to stand out from the competition and gain recognition. Similarly, if your target customers are preoccupied with the complexities and distractions of modern life, they may need more time or inclination to embrace your presented concept fully.

In such a scenario, it becomes crucial to identify an unmet need or niche in the crowded market to stand out from the competition and rise above the thorns. This can be achieved by conducting thorough market research to understand the customers' pain points, identifying gaps in the existing offerings, and leveraging your strengths to create a unique value proposition.

By doing so, you can differentiate your business from the existing players, establish a unique identity, and gain a competitive edge in the market. However, this requires a deep understanding of your industry, a willingness to adapt to changing market dynamics, and a relentless focus on delivering value to your customers.

Falling on Fertile Ground (Finding Your Niche)

Selecting the right niche in business is vital for long-term success. Just as fertile soil is essential for a seed to flourish, a favorable business environment is critical to developing an idea, product, or service. A niche market that aligns with your values and benefits and has a receptive audience can provide the optimal conditions for your business to thrive. It is crucial to identify this niche market and create a comprehensive strategy to target it effectively. You can achieve remarkable success beyond the initial investment by focusing on a specific audience with unmet needs and leveraging your strengths. This is like planting seeds in good soil that produce a hundred, sixty, or thirtyfold. Therefore, conducting thorough research and analysis to identify and target the right niche should be a priority for any business or individual looking to achieve sustainable success.

So, how does this relate to finding a niche in business development?

Identifying and aligning a niche is crucial to building a successful enterprise. To achieve this, one must comprehensively understand the market landscape and select terrain that complements their talents and strengths. It involves thorough research, analysis, and strategic planning to identify a market segment that is underserved or has unmet needs that align with your business's products or services. Focusing efforts on a lucrative and sustainable niche is crucial for success instead of wasting resources in areas that may yield insignificant results.

A niche market is characterized by its specificity and specialization, representing a particular market subset with unique characteristics and requirements that can drive customer loyalty. Businesses can tailor their offerings to meet their niche audience's needs and preferences by focusing on a particular segment. This approach allows the business to establish itself, gain experience, and build a solid foundation before turning to more significant opportunities to expand and thrive.

A well-chosen niche can give a business a competitive advantage. By focusing on a particular market segment, a successful business in a niche can leverage that success as a springboard for expansion. It may seek opportunities to diversify its product or service offerings or enter new markets. This expansion can be more strategic and less risky than conquering an entire industry. However, the business must be responsible for harvesting profits and reinvesting them in innovation and expansion to ensure continuous development and competitiveness.

To succeed in a niche market, businesses must be adaptable and resilient to respond to changes in market conditions, customer preferences, and competitive forces. Businesses in different niches may face other challenges and opportunities, so they must be vigilant and agile to respond to changes in their market environment. This adaptability is critical to long-term success in the specific market environment.

Let's look at some real-life actions as current examples.

Reliance Industries Limited (RIL)

RIL, founded by Dhirubhai Ambani in 1966, is one of India's largest conglomerates with diversified business interests, including petrochemicals, refining, telecommunications, retail, and digital services. RIL's success can be attributed to its ability to thrive in highly regulated and capital-intensive industries. The business strategically leveraged India's growing demand for energy and connectivity, investing significantly in sectors with long-term growth potential. RIL's success is a prime example of how navigating complex regulatory environments, investing in infrastructure, and identifying emerging market needs can lead to substantial growth and success.

Apple

Apple is a business that prioritizes fostering growth, as evidenced by its unwavering commitment to providing exceptional user experiences and continuously pushing the boundaries of product innovation. They invest heavily in research and development to ensure their products remain cutting-edge and ahead of the technological curve.

In summary, identifying and aligning a niche in business and creativity requires a thorough understanding of the market landscape, research, analysis, and strategic planning. A well-chosen niche can give a business a competitive advantage, and responsible harvesting of profits and reinvestment in innovation and expansion ensure continuous development and competitiveness. To succeed in their specific market environment, businesses must be adaptable and resilient to respond to market conditions, customer preferences, and competitive forces. By aligning your business strategy with the principles outlined in this parable, you can increase your chances of success and growth in your chosen niche, providing your business with a bountiful harvest.

The Priceless Pursuit

*"**A** merchant looking for fine pearls.*

When he found one of great value,

he went away and sold everything

he had and bought it."

Parable of the Pearl of Great Price
Mathew 13:45-46

The parable of "A merchant in search of fine pearls" is a timeless fount of wisdom that is a practical illustration of a business development strategy. The story tells us about a wise, astute businessperson always looking for rare and valuable opportunities, much like a pearl hunter searching for fine pearls. As the story goes, the merchant eventually finds a pearl of exceptional value, and without hesitation, he decides to liquidate all his assets to acquire it.

This parable underscores the quintessence of a strategic approach to business development. It highlights the significance of identifying and seizing remarkable opportunities that can lead to substantial growth and profitability. The story teaches us to make sacrifices for long-term success and make bold decisions, even if it means taking significant risks. The merchant's path, decisions, and actions are closely intertwined with the art of strategic business development.

The story of the merchant also exemplifies the importance of patience, persistence, and resilience in business development. The merchant had to be patient and persistent in his search for the fine pearl, and he had to be resilient in the face of setbacks and challenges. His unwavering commitment and dedication to his goal ultimately paid off.

Furthermore, the story of the merchant highlights the significance of a long-term perspective in business development. The merchant knew that acquiring the fine pearl was not just a short-term gain but a long-term investment that would yield significant returns in the future. This insight enabled him to make the sacrifices and bold decisions required to achieve his goal.

The parable of "A merchant in search of fine pearls" is an excellent source of guidance for anyone seeking to develop a successful business. It teaches us the importance of identifying and seizing remarkable opportunities, making bold decisions, being patient, persistent, and resilient in facing challenges, and maintaining a long-term perspective.

The Quest for Great Value

Identifying opportunities with great potential in business development is a challenging task that can be compared to discovering a priceless pearl. It requires a deep understanding of industry trends, market research, and a discerning eye to recognize high-quality prospects, partnerships, and ventures. Businesses must allocate their resources wisely for growth and development, just like the merchant who committed his entire fortune to the valuable pearl.

To achieve growth and success, businesses must consistently seek high-potential opportunities and identify the potential for development and profitability. This involves conducting comprehensive market research, analyzing competitors, identifying trends, recognizing unmet customer needs, and staying ahead of the competition.

Recognizing an opportunity's value is vital in today's highly competitive environment. This may require reassessing current assets and their reallocation to achieve strategic goals. By seeking out the "pearl" in the marketplace, businesses lay the foundation for success. Therefore, businesses must constantly be alert for such opportunities and invest their resources wisely to achieve growth and development objectives.

The Willingness to Invest

The parable of the merchant and the pearl is a powerful reminder of the importance of a well-planned strategic decision-making process. Rather than impulsively purchasing a valuable pearl, the merchant embarked on a thoughtful journey to ensure the acquisition was worth the cost. He carefully assessed the risks and rewards and ensured his investment was well-considered and aligned with his objectives.

This story highlights the critical role of judgment and evaluation in effective business development. Conducting comprehensive due diligence, assessing risks, conducting feasibility studies, and evaluating the long-term prospects of an opportunity are all essential steps before making strategic decisions. Such diligence can minimize the risk of costly errors and drive success in the business world.

To succeed in business development, it is crucial to conduct a thorough analysis of various opportunities, markets, and ventures and weigh their potential returns against their risks. The merchant's commitment to selling everything he owned to acquire the precious pearl illustrates the significance of investment and commitment to business development. This means dedicating resources, time, and effort to exploit the identified opportunity in the business world.

Effective business development strategies should be adaptable, dynamic, and driven by pursuing opportunities that align with long-term goals. A successful plan requires a willingness to commit capital, human resources, and energy to its pursuit. Strategic decision-making is the foundation of business success, and it is essential to prioritize it accordingly. The merchant's journey in this parable demonstrates that business opportunities can be seized and turned into profitable ventures with the right approach, careful planning, and thoughtful consideration.

Risk-Taking and Sacrifice

The parable of the pearl of great value is a powerful reminder of the lengths to which a business or an entrepreneur may need to go to seize a promising opportunity. The merchant in the parable demonstrated an unwavering commitment and readiness to make significant sacrifices, such as liquidating all his assets, to obtain the pearl. This highlights that successful business development requires a willingness to take calculated risks and make tough sacrifices.

In business, seizing a valuable opportunity often requires a significant investment of resources, capital, and personnel. To achieve their development objectives, businesses may need to reallocate resources, commit considerable capital, or redeploy personnel to capitalize on a promising opportunity. This may involve divesting from existing products or services, reallocating budgets, or expanding into new markets.

However, making these sacrifices and taking calculated risks can be challenging and require significant planning and strategic thinking. Businesses must weigh the potential benefits against the risks and consider the potential long-term impacts of their actions.

A well-conceived business development strategy requires a willingness to take risks and make sacrifices, along with careful planning and execution. Ultimately, those willing to take calculated risks and make tough sacrifices will succeed in the highly competitive business world.

Strategic Timing

The parable about the merchant and the pearl teaches us a valuable lesson about the significance of timing. Instead of hastily selling all his assets, the merchant made a well-informed decision based on the value of the pearl. This story holds immense relevance in business development, where timing is equally crucial. To succeed in the competitive corporate world, it is essential to seize opportunities when they are ripe and execute strategies with precision to maximize their potential. Recognizing the right time to act, making informed decisions based on sound judgment, and considering all the factors involved are imperative. Doing so can make the most of the opportunities and stay ahead of the competition. In conclusion, the parable emphasizes that timing is critical, and one must be patient, wise, and strategic to succeed in business.

The Pursuit of Excellence

The merchant in the parable is a powerful and enduring metaphor for the entrepreneurial spirit, embodying the ceaseless pursuit of excellence and perfection integral to any successful business endeavor. The merchant's relentless quest for a "fine pearl" underscores the importance of quality and excellence in the business world, emphasizing the critical role of market intelligence in fostering such attributes. Businesses must possess a deep and comprehensive understanding of their industry, competitors, and core value-creating factors to make informed business decisions. This requires a strategic approach to business development, one that is rooted in a commitment to excellence and a relentless drive to achieve success.

Striving for excellence across all aspects of a business, from products and services to operations and customer service, is the bedrock of any successful strategy. This requires setting precise goals, effectively allocating resources, and defining the necessary steps for success. Prioritizing the most promising opportunities over others is vital in business development, as it often proves more advantageous to pursue a single, high-value venture than to spread resources across several low-impact ones. Recognizing what has genuine value and potential is a vital part of this process, as is developing a comprehensive understanding of the market and the competitive landscape.

Ultimately, excellence is a powerful magnet for attracting customers and maintaining a competitive edge. By prioritizing quality and striving for excellence in all aspects of their business, businesses can position themselves for long-term success and growth, building strong and lasting relationships with their customers and creating a culture of innovation and excellence that drives their ongoing success.

Vision and Long-Term Perspective

The merchant we refer to possesses a clear and well-defined long-term vision, which he was deeply committed to and believed in. His unwavering conviction in the enduring value of pearls motivated him to make strategic investments that would yield a future of more excellent value rather than being driven by the prospect of quick, short-term gains. His success resulted from his determination to build a prosperous business to generate substantial profits and thrive in the long run.

In business development, having a clear vision and adopting a long-term perspective is essential for achieving sustainable success. Accomplished businesses recognize that specific opportunities require patience, sustained commitment, and the ability to make strategic choices. These choices should align with the overarching objectives of an organization, and decisions should be made with an understanding of their potential impact over time.

Building a prosperous business demands time and patience; not all opportunities are immediately discernible. It requires one to be able to identify opportunities that have the potential to grow and sustain the business in the long run. Strategic choices ought to be guided by a consideration of sustainability and growth rather than short-term gains. A steadfast commitment to long-term goals is a crucial driver of success, and businesses that prioritize long-term growth are more likely to thrive in the long run.

Adaptability and Flexibility

Based on the story of a merchant who acquires a valuable pearl, the parable does not provide explicit details on how the merchant obtained the pearl or the extent of his travels. However, it does offer valuable insights into the adaptive and flexible nature of the merchant's approach. The merchant's ability to adjust his strategies and adapt to the changing market dynamics was a critical factor in his success. This is a testament to the importance of adaptability and flexibility in business development.

Consider the following real-life actions as tangible examples.

Flipkart

Flipkart, founded by Sachin Bansal and Binny Bansal in 2007, recognized the untapped potential of e-commerce in India. The business identified the opportunity to create an online marketplace that could serve the needs of India's growing consumer base. Flipkart started as an online bookstore and gradually expanded to offer various products. The business's strategic approach and early-mover advantage in e-commerce allowed it to capture a significant market share. Flipkart's ability to recognize and act on the potential for e-commerce growth in India led to its substantial success, eventually attracting the attention of global e-commerce giant Walmart, which acquired a majority stake in the business.

Biocon

Biocon, a biopharmaceutical business, recognized the global demand for affordable, high-quality biotech products. The business focused on research and development and became a pioneer in the production of biosimilars. Biocon identified opportunities in the global market for biopharmaceuticals and seized them by forming strategic partnerships and collaborations with multinational pharmaceutical businesses, leading to significant growth and profitability.

In the fast-paced business world, various factors, such as technological advancements and evolving customer preferences, can challenge businesses. Achieving sustainable business development requires businesses to remain flexible and willing to adjust their strategies in response to new information or challenges. By doing so, businesses can capitalize on growth opportunities and stay competitive in their respective markets.

To design a successful business development strategy, aligning business strategies with basic principles is vital. This approach is like the merchant's quest for the precious pearl that resulted in a valuable acquisition. This equates to achieving strategic objectives, market dominance, or gaining a competitive advantage in the business world. Businesses seeking and leveraging high-value opportunities are better poised to attain significant growth and success. Businesses need to identify and evaluate opportunities in their respective markets continually. By doing so, businesses can remain competitive and achieve their business objectives.

The Eternal Wisdom of Diligence

"*A* landowner who went out early in the morning

to hire workers for his vineyard.

He agreed to pay them a denarius for the day

and sent them into his vineyard.

"About nine in the morning, he went out

and saw others standing

in the marketplace doing nothing.

He told them, 'You also go and work in my vineyard,
and I will pay you whatever is right.' So, they went.

"He went out again about noon and about three
in the afternoon and did the same thing.
At about five in the afternoon, he went out and found
still others standing around. He asked them,

'Why have you been standing here
all day long doing nothing?'
"'Because no one has hired us,' they answered.
"He said to them, 'You also go
and work in my vineyard.'

"When evening came,
the owner of the vineyard said to his foreman,
'Call the workers and pay them their wages,
beginning with the last ones hired
and going on to the first.'
"The workers who were hired
about five in the afternoon

came, and each received a denarius.

So when those came who were hired first,

they expected to receive more.

But each one of them also received a denarius.

When they received it, they began to grumble

against the landowner.

'These who were hired last worked only one hour,'

they said, 'and you have made them equal to us who

have borne the burden of the work

and the heat of the day.'

"But he answered one of them,

'I am not being unfair to you, friend.

Didn't you agree to work for a denarius?

Take your pay and go.

I want to give the one who was hired last

the same as I gave you.

Don't I have the right to do

what I want with my own money?

Or are you envious because I am generous?'

"So, the last will be first, and the first will be last."

Parable of the Workers in the Vineyard
Mathew 20:1-16

- A denarius was the usual daily wage of a day laborer.

Developing an effective business strategy is a complex process that requires careful planning, deep foresight, and equitable practices. One instructive story that highlights the significance of fairness, the perceived value of effort and reward, and the establishment of a culture of justice in business development and management is the parable of the vineyard owner and his workers.

The owner's decision to pay all workers equally regardless of their hiring time presents a challenge for business leaders to devise strategies that guarantee equitable compensation and recognition for all employees. This narrative is an inspiring framework for exploring how modern businesses can integrate benevolence, manage expectations, and promote a fair environment that values all employees equally.

The parable provides profound inspiration and guidance for developing innovative strategies that enhance organizational growth and harmony. It emphasizes the importance of treating employees fairly, as it promotes a positive and productive work environment. Therefore, business leaders must learn from this story and implement equitable practices that ensure employees are compensated and recognized reasonably in their organizations.

Talent Acquisition and Inclusivity

The parable of the landowner who hired previously overlooked workers for his vineyard highlights the crucial role of identifying and integrating untapped talent into the workforce. This narrative emphasizes the importance of adopting an inclusive approach while seeking out potential employees in the business domain. It is essential to broaden the recruitment horizons and consider candidates from diverse backgrounds, experiences, and skill sets to foster innovation and problem-solving capabilities.

Bringing new hires on board at a later stage can offer fresh perspectives and ideas that are beneficial to the business. An open-minded approach to recruitment encourages businesses to explore untapped talent, which can lead to a more diverse pool of employees, new ideas, and perspectives. This, in turn, promotes growth and development in the business.

Moreover, ensuring equal opportunities and fair remuneration for all employees fosters a positive work environment while reducing inequities. Including individuals with diverse backgrounds and experiences leads to a more diverse and inclusive culture that promotes innovation, creativity, and productivity. It is, therefore, crucial for businesses to prioritize diversity and inclusivity in their recruitment and employment practices.

Flexibility in Resource Allocation

A business's success is primarily determined by its ability to optimize resources and be adaptable. Businesses capable of responding to changing needs and circumstances are more efficient in resource allocation and have better productivity. Adaptability enables organizations to adjust their strategies and workforce to evolving circumstances, seize new opportunities, and optimize resources, leading to greater competitiveness in a dynamic business environment.

The importance of adaptability can be illustrated through the example of a landowner who hires additional workers at different times of the day depending on the needs of the farm. This flexible approach to resource allocation enables the landowner to maximize available resources, even if they are available at unconventional times. By being open to changes in strategies and approaches, businesses can respond effectively to market demands and remain competitive.

To develop a successful business, businesses must remain receptive to new ideas and talent. This means being open to hiring new talent when necessary and making the most of available resources. A flexible approach to business development is essential for responding to changing needs and circumstances. It is a reminder that businesses should be willing to adjust their strategies and workforce to evolving circumstances.

Adaptability is a critical factor in the success of any business. Businesses open to changes in strategies and approaches can seize new opportunities, optimize resources, and achieve greater competitiveness. By being flexible in their approach to business development and making the most of available resources, businesses can respond effectively to market demands and remain successful.

Fair Compensation and Agreements

The decision taken by the landowner to pay equal wages to all workers, regardless of the number of hours worked, is a highly commendable step towards ensuring transparency in labor contracts and promoting fair pay. In the corporate domain, providing equitable compensation and benefits to all employees, irrespective of their position or experience, can help build a more cohesive and motivated workforce, contributing to the organization's growth. Treating every employee and partner equally, regardless of their contributions, can create a positive work environment with improved morale, trust, loyalty, and commitment. Business leaders should make sure that they offer competitive compensation packages to attract and retain skilled employees, as this can also help strengthen the organization's reputation. Maintaining integrity and fulfilling commitments is crucial in establishing trust within the organization, with business partners, and with customers. When employers treat their employees with respect and fairness, it often results in mutual dedication and commitment to the organization, leading to increased productivity and better performance.

Addressing Employee Concerns

The parable of the workers in the vineyard is a classic example of how high expectations can lead to dissatisfaction and conflicts. The parable tells the story of how the workers hired early in the day expected to receive more wages than those employed later, even though they all agreed to work for the same daily wage. The landowner, however, addressed their concerns by explaining his decision to pay them all a fair wage, regardless of the time they started working. This parable offers valuable insights into managing entitlements and expectations in a business context.

To manage entitlements effectively, it is crucial to establish clear expectations and agreements with employees. This can be achieved by communicating compensation structures, performance metrics, and opportunities for advancement to avoid disputes and dissatisfaction. Clear communication and transparency around rewards and compensation can help prevent misunderstandings and conflicts.

Listening to employees' concerns and communicating clearly and actively is essential. Addressing complaints or questions and keeping them informed of any changes or developments in the business is crucial. Clear communication contributes to a positive working environment and builds trust between employees and management. Open dialogue can help manage expectations and resolve disputes.

In a business context, managing expectations is critical, particularly regarding salary negotiations, project timelines, or return on investment. Setting clear and realistic expectations is essential to avoid misunderstandings and conflicts. Treating all employees fairly, regardless of their seniority, can motivate them to contribute to the business's success. Businesses can learn from this by implementing performance-based reward systems. Recognizing and rewarding employees based on their contributions can increase motivation and productivity. Moreover, providing training and career development opportunities shows employees that the business values their skills and is invested in their growth.

The parable of the workers in the vineyard teaches us the importance of managing entitlements and expectations fairly and transparently. By establishing clear expectations and agreements, communicating effectively, and treating all employees fairly, businesses can avoid conflicts and increase motivation and productivity. It is crucial to listen to employees' concerns, provide growth opportunities, and recognize their contributions to the business's success.

Generosity and Corporate Social Responsibility

The landowner's response to the dispute was generous and marked by his emphasis on his right to be so. He underscored the importance of corporate social responsibility and generosity's role in business. His great act resolved the dispute and earned him the workers' loyalty. His leadership style set an exemplary standard for other leaders to follow. Acts of kindness such as charitable initiatives, the equitable treatment of employees, and customer rewards can foster goodwill in the community and industry and bolster a business's reputation. Encouraging generosity and teamwork within a business can lead to increased collaboration and cohesion, promoting business growth. It is essential to acknowledge and value the hard work of all employees, regardless of their position or tenure, as this can create a positive and motivated work culture. Generosity in business can lead to a more devoted and driven workforce through training, support, and perks. A long-term approach centered on nurturing talent is vital to sustainable growth. Leaders resolve disputes by adopting a generous and magnanimous approach to business and creating a culture of collaboration, loyalty, and development.

Long-term Vision

Effective leadership in the context of landownership shares similarities with corporate governance and property rights. It involves granting autonomy to landowners to use their resources as they deem fit while requiring competent leaders to make difficult decisions that serve the organization's greater good, even if they face criticism. The ability to make informed and strategic decisions is crucial for the long-term success of any business. Leaders must have a clear vision and purpose to guide their actions while considering ethical and legal obligations.

To achieve sustainable growth, businesses must invest in research, development, and employee training, even if they await immediate returns. These investments can lay the foundation for future success and help businesses stay ahead of their competitors. To make effective decisions, leaders must exercise patience and wait for the right moment to undertake strategic investments or decisions. Hasty decisions can lead to adverse outcomes and hinder a business's growth.

Successful leadership in land ownership, corporate governance, and property rights requires strategic thinking, a clear vision, ethical and legal considerations, and patience to make informed decisions that serve the organization's greater good.

Hierarchy and Recognition

The parable of the vineyard is a powerful tale that teaches a crucial lesson in business development. It emphasizes that seniority alone should not be the basis for organizational hierarchy and recognition. Instead, those who contribute the most and work the hardest should be acknowledged and advanced, regardless of their position or rank. This principle is fundamental in the dynamic and ever-evolving business landscape, where success and recognition can shift over time. Emerging start-ups can disrupt established industries, and even long-established businesses may lose their competitive edge.

Let's take a look at some real-life actions as present-day examples.

Buffer's Transparent Salary Formula

Buffer is a business that specializes in social media management and is renowned for its transparent salary formula. The business believes in fairness and equity and openly shares its method of calculating employee salaries. This approach has garnered significant attention and admiration from the industry.

The Body Shop Fair Trade Agreements

The Body Shop sources many of its critical ingredients through fair trade agreements, ensuring that the communities involved in production receive fair wages and fair treatment. The business significantly emphasizes employee welfare, offering its staff comprehensive benefits and training opportunities. They have policies to support a diverse and inclusive workforce.

To achieve sustainable growth, business leaders must remain open to new ideas, innovations, and emerging talent that can offer a fresh perspective and lead to a turnaround. The parable of the vineyard imparts valuable insights for businesses aspiring to achieve this goal. By embracing diversity in all forms, ensuring equitable compensation, maintaining flexibility, acknowledging contributions, fostering generosity, and pursuing long-term objectives, businesses can formulate innovative business strategies that align with the parable's fairness, diligence, and kindness principles.

By adopting these principles, businesses can position themselves to prosper and promote harmonious relationships within their organization. It is important to note that, just as in the parable, the last can become the first in the business world. This means that by valuing hard work, innovation, and collaboration, businesses can create a culture that rewards and recognizes excellence, regardless of an individual's position or rank. Ultimately, the parable of the vineyard teaches us that by valuing people over titles, businesses can achieve sustainable growth and success over the long term.

A Blueprint

"Again, it will be like a man going on a journey,

who called his servants and entrusted his wealth

to them. To one he gave five bags of gold,

to another two bags, and to another one bag,

each according to his ability.

Then he went on his journey.

The man who had received five bags of gold

went at once, put his money to work

and gained five more bags.

So also, the one with two bags of gold

gained two more.

But the man who had received one bag went off,

dug a hole in the ground

and hid his master's money.

"After a long time, the master of those servants

returned and settled accounts with them.

The man who had received five bags of gold

brought the other five.

'Master,' he said, 'you entrusted me

with five bags of gold.

See, I have gained five more. "His master replied,

'Well done, good and faithful servant!

You have been faithful with a few things;

I will put you in charge of many things.

Come and share your master's happiness!'

"The man with two bags of gold also came.

'Master,' he said, 'you entrusted

me with two bags of gold;

see, I have gained two more.'

"His master replied, 'Well done, good

and faithful servant!

You have been faithful with a few things;

I will put you in charge of many things.

Come and share your master's happiness!'

"Then the man who had received

one bag of gold came.

'Master,' he said, 'I knew that you are a hard man,

harvesting where you have not sown and

gathering where you have not scattered seed.

So, I was afraid and went out

and hid your gold in the ground.

See, here is what belongs to you.'

"His master replied, 'You wicked, lazy servant!

So you knew that I harvest

where I have not sown and

gather where I have not scattered seed?

Well then, you should have put my money on deposit

with the bankers, so that when I returned,

I would have received it back with interest.'

" 'So take the bag of gold from him and

give it to the one who has ten bags.

For whoever has will be given more,

and they will have an abundance.

Whoever does not have,

even what they have will be taken from them.

And throw that worthless servant outside,

into the darkness,

where there will be weeping and gnashing of teeth.' "

Parable of the Talents
Mathew 25:14-30

- A Talent was worth about 20 years of a day laborer's wage.

In today's hyper-competitive business world, effective management and the development of talents are crucial for achieving success. The parable of talents, a timeless narrative, is relevant to business development across generations. It encapsulates the essence of entrepreneurship, investment, and personal growth, highlighting the importance of utilizing one's skills and resources to achieve growth, capitalize on opportunities, and maximize potential.

The parable tells the story of a master who entrusts his servants with varying amounts of talent, a currency in ancient times. The servants' responses and attitudes towards these talents have far-reaching consequences for their future. This parable provides a plethora of wisdom that can empower individuals and organizations to move from scarcity to abundance. It helps us comprehend that business development is not just about accumulating wealth but also about being a responsible steward of one's talents and enjoying the fruits of one's labor.

The timeless wisdom of this parable on stewardship and investment contains valuable lessons for modern entrepreneurs, managers, and business leaders. It provides insights on leveraging one's talents to achieve growth, capitalize on opportunities, and maximize potential while being a responsible steward of one's resources. The parable emphasizes investing in oneself, taking calculated risks, and nurturing one's talents to achieve long-term success. It also highlights the significance of trust, accountability, and responsibility in achieving business success. By utilizing the lessons from this parable, individuals and organizations can develop a culture of growth, innovation, and excellence that can help them stand out in today's competitive business landscape.

Talent Allocation Reflects Leadership Wisdom

The Parable of the Talents is a powerful tale that offers a valuable lesson regarding business development. According to the story, a master distributed talents among his servants based on their abilities, and each servant was responsible for managing and investing the talents they received. The story highlights the importance of talent allocation and the trust entrepreneurs or leaders place in their teams.

Businesses must recognize each team member's unique strengths and resources to achieve maximum productivity and success. Following the example of the master in the parable, wise leaders must allocate resources, responsibilities, and opportunities according to the capabilities of their team members. This enables practical task assignments and ensures everyone contributes to their full potential.

The Parable of the Talents also emphasizes taking risks and seizing opportunities. In the story, the servants who invested and multiplied their talents were rewarded, while the servant who buried his talent was punished. This illustrates the need for entrepreneurs and leaders to identify and pursue opportunities that have the potential to yield significant returns.

Recognizing and leveraging individual talents results in higher productivity, success, and a positive work environment. Therefore, organizations must recognize the talents and capabilities of their employees, partners, and stakeholders to achieve these benefits. By doing so, businesses can create a trust, collaboration, and innovation culture that drives growth and prosperity.

Risk-taking and Initiative Are Rewarded

The parable of the talents conveys a powerful message about the significance of investing resources to promote growth. In this story, two servants were given different amounts of talents - five and two, respectively. Both chose to invest their resources immediately and managed to make them grow. They demonstrated initiative and a willingness to take calculated risks, a fundamental business development principle.

This principle is vital in entrepreneurship and leadership, where seizing opportunities and innovating by responding to market trends, customer needs, and new technologies is essential. In today's dynamic business environment, waiting for the ideal moment can lead to missed opportunities. Entrepreneurs and leaders must be willing to step out of their comfort zones, invest in their ventures, and take calculated risks to achieve growth and success.

However, it is critical to make informed decisions and manage risks wisely. Investing in one's initiative is not a guarantee of success. It requires a deep understanding of market trends, customer needs, and available resources. Calculated risks supported by research and analysis can result in significant victories. Entrepreneurs and leaders must be prepared to make informed decisions and manage risks effectively.

Ultimately, the parable of the talents serves as a reminder that investing in growth requires initiative, calculated risk-taking, and a willingness to innovate. It highlights the importance of taking action and investing resources in opportunities that have the potential to generate growth and higher profitability. Entrepreneurs and leaders can create a roadmap for business expansion and success by taking calculated risks and managing them wisely.

Diligence and Accountability Matter

In the parables, a master entrusted his possessions to his servants and went on a journey. Upon his return to settle accounts, he praised the servants who had multiplied their talents, commending them for their dedication and trustworthiness. This narrative, often viewed in commerce, highlights the importance of accountability and perseverance in achieving success.

Whether you are a business executive, an entrepreneur, or an employee, it is essential to prioritize transparency, ethical conduct, and responsible resource allocation. To maintain the trust and credibility crucial to long-term success, tracking progress, monitoring key performance indicators, demonstrating a solid work ethic, and being accountable to stakeholders is necessary. Achievements in the business world often lead to recognition, dependability, and increased opportunities.

Establishing a reputation for reliability, competence, and ethical conduct can pave the way for partnerships, collaborations, and business growth. In today's world, where competition is fierce, and the stakes are high, prioritizing accountability, transparency, and ethical conduct is more important than ever. You can build lasting relationships with customers, clients, and partners and achieve your desired success.

Fear and Inaction Lead to Stagnation

The parable of the servant who received a talent is a powerful illustration of the negative consequences of being immobilized by fear and indecision. The story serves as a reminder that failure to take action can lead to stagnation, lack of achievement, and impede growth in the business world. It is, therefore, important for leaders to cultivate a culture that values and encourages innovation, calculated risk-taking, and a growth mindset. Rather than burying opportunities, leaders should strive to nurture and multiply them and make informed decisions to overcome challenges and avoid complacency through inaction.

To achieve success, it is crucial to assess risks carefully and evaluate potential outcomes without being paralyzed by fear. Failure is often viewed as a negative outcome, but it can be an integral part of the learning process and essential for personal and professional development. Leaders should encourage their teams to take calculated risks, learn from their mistakes, and use those lessons to drive future success. By fostering a culture of growth, innovation, and calculated risk-taking, leaders can ensure that their teams are well-prepared to tackle challenges and capitalize on opportunities in a rapidly changing business environment.

Maximizing Resources Through Investment

The prudent management of resources is a cornerstone of effective business development, as illustrated by the parable of the servant who buried the talent instead of investing it. This story emphasizes the importance of seizing opportunities and allocating resources wisely to achieve a return on investment. The principle of multiplication is central to business development, and businesses must continually evaluate their strategies and initiatives to ensure optimal returns on investment. This applies to all types of assets, including financial capital, intellectual property, and human capital. Enterprises must proactively seek ways to enhance the value of their investments, whether by reallocating resources, diversifying products and services, or entering new markets.

To remain competitive and profitable, businesses must prioritize smart investments, strategic partnerships, and innovation as key drivers of resource optimization. They should not only preserve their assets but also explore ways to leverage them to generate returns that enhance the overall value of their operations. This requires continuously evaluating and refining business practices to ensure that resources are used efficiently and effectively. By doing so, businesses can maximize the value of their assets and position themselves for long-term success in a rapidly changing business environment.

The Law of Accumulation or Abundance

The parable mentioned in the text portrays a significant concept of "to everyone who has, more will be given." It narrates a story where a master entrusts his property to his servants and goes on a journey. He gives five talents to one servant, two to another, and one to the third, based on their potential and abilities. The first two servants invest and trade with the talents and double their value, whereas the third servant buries his talent in the ground.

Upon the master's return, he rewards the first two servants for their resourcefulness, but the third servant faces punishment for his inaction and fear of losing the talent. The master removes one talent from the unproductive servant and gives it to the one who already possesses ten talents.

This parable exemplifies the law of accumulation in business, which implies that individuals who effectively manage and grow their resources will receive even more or may attract more opportunities and growth. It accentuates the significance of having an initiative and a growth mindset. It encourages individuals and organizations to maximize available opportunities and develop their resources and capabilities for tremendous success.

Successful businesses often experience a compounding effect, where growth leads to further growth. By applying this law of abundance in their operations, businesses can create a positive cycle of growth and development that propels them towards greater heights of success.

Consequences of Inaction

The parable of the unproductive servant serves as a cautionary tale for individuals and businesses alike. It illustrates the grave consequences of inactivity, neglect, and poor stewardship. The servant was penalized for failing to use the resources entrusted in the parable. Similarly, inactivity can lead to missed opportunities for growth and success, which can have deep-seated impacts in a competitive marketplace.

In the fast-paced and ever-changing business landscape, businesses that fail to capitalize on opportunities, adjust to changing circumstances, or explore new growth prospects can face a loss of market share, setbacks, and even the possibility of quitting the business. Therefore, it is vital to consistently seek opportunities for growth and innovation to stay caught up. Taking the initiative, making responsible decisions, and maximizing available resources and opportunities are critical to achieving growth and success.

The competitive business landscape demands initiative, and businesses that fail to act may become irrelevant or isolated, overshadowed by their more proactive competitors. Neglecting these responsibilities can lead to negative consequences that businesses must avoid at all costs. Hence, the parable of talent is a profound narrative that significantly impacts every aspect of business development.

Businesses need to be proactive in identifying and capitalizing on opportunities for growth and development. This involves leveraging available resources, investing in research and development, fostering innovation, and creating a culture of continuous improvement. Successful business development is about making profits and optimizing the potential of individuals and organizations to achieve their objectives and positively impact the world.

Real-life examples are essential to understand concepts. Let me show you some present-day actions to help you get a better grasp. They will undoubtedly make the topic more relatable and more accessible to comprehend.

Warren Buffett

Warren Buffett, a well-known investor, is an excellent example of multiplying resources. He invests in businesses with the potential for long-term growth, allowing his investments to compound over time. His approach to investing reflects the Parable of the Talents, which emphasizes the importance of using resources wisely to achieve long-term success.

Amazon

Amazon has a remarkable track record of seizing opportunities and taking calculated risks, which has helped it become one of the most successful businesses in the world. Starting as an online bookstore, Amazon has expanded its business to diverse markets such as cloud computing and online retail. Amazon's agility and willingness to embrace new opportunities have been vital to its success in an ever-changing business landscape.

In conclusion, the parable of talent emphasizes the importance of taking the initiative, embracing change, and maximizing available resources and opportunities. By incorporating these principles, entrepreneurs and leaders can surmount the challenges of the contemporary business world and work towards achieving long-term success and prosperity. The lesson from the parable is clear: inaction can lead to stagnation and missed growth opportunities, whereas taking the initiative can lead to expansion, higher profits, and long-term success.

7

The Wealth That Endures

"The ground of a certain rich man yielded an

abundant harvest. He thought to himself,

'What shall I do? I have no place to store my crops.'

"Then he said, 'This is what I'll do.

I will tear down my barns and build bigger ones,

and there I will store my surplus grain.

And I'll say to myself,

"You have plenty of grain laid up for many years.

Take life easy; eat, drink, and be merry." '

"But God said to him, 'You fool!

This very night your life will be demanded from you.

Then who will get

what you have prepared for yourself?'

"This is how it will be with whoever stores up

things for themselves but is not rich toward God."

Parable of the Rich Fool
Luke 12:16-21

The maxim "The soil of a rich man yielded a rich harvest" is a timeless reminder of the importance of financial planning and wealth management. The story's protagonist was wealthy and had a bountiful harvest, but his success was short-lived due to his ambition, shortsightedness, and preference for immediate gain over long-term prosperity. This narrative is just as relevant today as it was in the past, highlighting the need for individuals to prioritize strategic and sustainable practices for cultivating long-term abundance instead of focusing solely on accumulating wealth. The tale's lessons offer valuable insights to entrepreneurs and leaders alike, who can use them to develop sound business strategies that promote ethical and sustainable practices. By focusing on sustainable practices, businesses can ensure long-term success while contributing to a more equitable and sustainable society. The story also reinforces the importance of balancing short-term and long-term goals and cultivating a mindset of abundance rather than scarcity. Ultimately, the maxim is a powerful reminder that financial success is not achieved through luck or short-term thinking but through careful planning and a commitment to sustainable practices.

Cultivate a Vision for Sustainable Growth

Developing a successful business strategy is a complex and multi-dimensional process that requires careful planning and execution. At the core of this process is having a clear vision that extends beyond immediate financial gains. Starting by assessing your current financial situation, setting clear goals, and creating an appropriate budget that aligns with your values is crucial.

It is essential to note that a successful business strategy is not solely about accumulating wealth. The rich man's parable is an excellent example of how a plan focusing only on financial gain can neglect other crucial dimensions of life and business development. Such an approach does not guarantee long-term sustainability and can harm the business's overall success.

Instead, pursuing a vision prioritizing sustainable growth, innovation, and long-term value creation is crucial. A sustainable business strategy must be innovative and adaptable to changing market conditions, customer needs, and emerging trends. Continuously reviewing your plan and assessing how it aligns with your vision is paramount to this process.

It is important to remember that business success is not just about accumulating wealth but also about positively impacting society. Hence, developing a business strategy that aligns with your values and contributes to the betterment of society is a crucial aspect of long-term success. It requires a commitment to ethical and social responsibility, including sustainable practices, fair treatment of employees, and environmentally friendly policies.

A successful business strategy requires a clear vision, careful planning, and execution. Prioritizing sustainable growth, innovation, and the creation of long-term value while remaining committed to ethical and social responsibility is crucial to achieving long-term success.

Recognizing Abundance

A wealthy individual's land is often blessed with a bountiful harvest, symbolizing prosperity, success, and abundance in the business world. This achievement is a crucial milestone that all entrepreneurs and business entities aspire to attain, as it signifies the availability of ample resources and opportunities for growth and expansion. To reach this stage, businesses must remain vigilant and adaptable to emerging market trends, consumer demands, and innovative technologies. It requires a constant effort to stay ahead of the competition and maintain a competitive edge in a rapidly evolving business landscape. Thus, realizing abundance indicates a crucial moment in business development, where the focus shifts towards sustained growth and long-term success.

Evaluate and Optimize Resources

When a person becomes wealthy, it is natural to desire even greater success. However, deciding to demolish existing structures and construct larger ones may indicate excessive ambition. It is essential to balance ambition and caution when expanding a business. Rapid expansion without appropriate planning may lead to instability and risk. Therefore, an effective business development strategy prioritizes steady, controlled growth that aligns with the business's capabilities and market demands.

Businesses must maximize their resources by assessing their financial, human, and intellectual resources to achieve optimal growth. This appraisal should inform decisions concerning expansion, investment, and resource allocation. Evaluating the business's financial position and the resources required to support growth is crucial. The business's human resources should also be assessed to ensure that it has the necessary talent to support growth and that the staff is adequately trained to carry out their roles effectively. Additionally, intellectual resources, such as patents and trade secrets, should be evaluated to ensure they are utilized effectively.

Once the business's resources have been evaluated, a growth plan should be developed that considers the business's capabilities and market demands. The plan should include a timeline for growth and a strategy for managing risks associated with expansion. It is also essential to consider the impact of development on the business's culture and values.

Businesses should approach growth cautiously and develop a well-planned growth strategy that aligns with their capabilities and market demands. By maximizing their resources and managing risks associated with expansion, businesses can achieve steady, controlled growth and avoid instability and risk.

The Peril of Short-Term Thinking

The parable of the wealthy man who sought to store his surplus grain and live a life of leisure serves as a prime example of falling into the trap of abundance. The narrative highlights the dangers of complacency and shortsightedness resulting from unexpected economic profits or windfalls, leading individuals to assume that prosperity will persist indefinitely. However, the wealthy man is not criticized for his wealth in the story but for failing to plan for the future.

The story is a cautionary tale, reminding us that life is unpredictable and things can change rapidly. The wealthy man yearned to indulge in a life of leisure without comprehending the risks inherent in his immoderate behavior. The lesson is that excessive accumulation can lead to financial ruin and discontentment, leaving individuals vulnerable to unforeseen obstacles.

In business development, it is tempting to prioritize immediate gains and swift profits over long-term planning and sustainability. However, genuine success often results from establishing enduring relationships with customers, employees, and partners. A business prioritizing short-term gains over long-term planning may miss valuable opportunities and underutilize its assets.

Modern financial planning emphasizes diversification and strategic investing to mitigate risks and ensure long-term growth. Businesses can thrive and prosper by prioritizing sustainable strategies and cultivating enduring relationships.

Diversify and Adapt

The parable of the affluent man highlights the disastrous consequences of a lack of contingency planning and risk management. Man's failure to diversify his wealth and instead concentrate all his resources on building larger barns was a prime example of 'putting all one's eggs in one basket.' In contrast, the principles of wealth management emphasize the significance of diversifying investments to mitigate risk and maximize returns. This can entail investing in research and development, expanding the team, venturing into new markets, or diversifying the product/service offerings.

In the context of business development, diversification and risk mitigation strategies are of vital importance. Overreliance on a single product, market, or customer can lead to disastrous consequences. Instead of accumulating resources, businesses should diversify their investments and adapt to changing circumstances to ensure long-term sustainability. The rich man's fatal blunder was his failure to anticipate the unpredictability of life. A sound business strategy involves scenario planning and risk assessments to be prepared for unforeseen challenges.

To minimize risk and foster resilience to economic fluctuations, diversification of products, services, and markets is a fundamental principle of wealth preservation. A diversified portfolio can help reduce the impact of adverse events on the overall business performance and provide a cushion to absorb unforeseen shocks. This can help businesses thrive in uncertain times and stay competitive in the long run. Therefore, businesses must adopt a diversified approach to wealth management and risk mitigation to ensure long-term sustainability and success.

Focus on Value Creation

The parable teaches us a valuable lesson about prioritizing customer satisfaction and contributing to the betterment of society as a whole. The rich man in the story focuses on accumulating wealth for his pleasure. In contrast, businesses should be more concerned with providing value to their customers and the community. By doing so, businesses can foster long-term profitability and customer loyalty.

One effective way of achieving this goal is by making wise investments in assets that have the potential to appreciate over time, such as stocks, real estate, or starting a business. This can generate significant returns and provide a strong foundation for future growth.

Moreover, individuals have the power to make a lasting impact on their community and the world by engaging in thoughtful estate planning, charitable giving, or other meaningful activities. By doing so, they can contribute to causes that align with their values and help those in need.

A comprehensive business development strategy should also incorporate ways to give back to the community. This can involve identifying ways in which your products or services can address social issues, enhance people's lives, or meet the needs of your target audience. Doing so can establish a strong reputation as a socially responsible business and build a loyal customer base that shares your values.

In summary, the parable serves as a reminder that businesses should strive to create value for their customers and society. By making wise investments, engaging in charitable giving, and prioritizing social responsibility, businesses can achieve long-term success and positively impact the world.

Responsible Wealth Management

Businesses must adopt responsible asset management practices and avoid short-sighted approaches, as illustrated by the case of wealthy individuals. Effective financial planning requires accumulating wealth and creating a lasting legacy for future generations and the community. Achieving financial success is about generating income and knowing how to use it effectively.

Evaluating assets and understanding how to manage them is critical to financial planning. It requires balancing present needs with future security, including estate planning to ensure the distribution of assets according to individual wishes in unforeseen circumstances.

A sustainable financial strategy involves diversification and risk management, reinvestment in the business, philanthropic efforts, and the maintenance of financial stability. Planning for the unexpected and considering the well-being of employees, stakeholders, and the community are also essential elements of financial planning.

Financial success combines a sense of purpose and moral responsibility, resulting in a deeper form of prosperity. It serves as a reminder that careful management of resources leads to overall wealth. Therefore, businesses must adopt a responsible asset management approach that recognizes the importance of a sound financial strategy.

Build Ethical Foundations

The parable is an ageless tale that serves as a reminder that material wealth alone cannot provide a fulfilling life. The story emphasizes the dangers of being consumed by greed and highlights the significance of striking a balance in one's financial pursuits. The narrative takes a twist when the wealthy man faces his mortality, a poignant reminder of life's unpredictability and the importance of being prepared for unforeseen events.

Incorporating risk management and insurance into our financial planning is crucial. It helps us safeguard our economic future against unforeseen events that can disrupt even the most carefully crafted financial plans. We must align effective wealth management with our personal values and social responsibility. Investing in ethical and sustainable businesses and engaging with the community can contribute significantly to our wealth. Businesses that integrate ethical, social, and environmental considerations into their strategies tend to be more resilient and prosperous in the long run, making it clear that financial success must always be balanced with ethical principles and social consciousness.

Furthermore, businesses should establish their foundation on ethics and social responsibility, as it protects against unforeseen consequences and enhances brand reputation and customer trust. In this light, it is evident that effective financial planning involves more than just accumulating wealth; it requires aligning our values with our financial goals while ensuring social responsibility.

Prioritize Long-term Sustainability

In the process of developing a comprehensive business strategy, it is crucial to place a higher emphasis on achieving long-term sustainability rather than just focusing on short-term gains. This is because wealth can be fleeting, as evidenced by the famous fable of the wealthy man. Therefore, it is of utmost importance to create a well-thought-out wealth plan that can withstand the test of time and be passed on to future generations, ensuring your business's continued success and prosperity. This involves considering market trends, customer demands, technological advancements, and financial stability to create a solid foundation for your business that can weather any challenges or obstacles. Ultimately, prioritizing long-term sustainability over short-term gains is critical in building a successful and enduring business that can thrive for years.

The Value of Continuous Learning

"A Rich Man's Reason" teaches us a valuable lesson about the importance of humility and the willingness to learn. The wealthy man's arrogance closed his eyes to the realities of life and business, and he failed to recognize the benefits that wise counsel could have brought him. The story emphasizes the critical role of collaborating with financial experts who can provide well-informed advice while making crucial decisions. It is vital to stay current with financial trends and tailor strategies accordingly to ensure alignment with objectives and the dynamic economic landscape.

Accomplished business developers recognize that maintaining humility is essential, even in the face of success. The importance of constantly adapting and learning from mistakes is also emphasized. The message conveyed by "A Rich Man's Reason" is of immense significance to businesses navigating the complex terrain of development and growth. By embracing a strategy rooted in prudence, long-term vision, and ethical conduct, businesses can avoid the pitfalls that ensnared the rich man in the story. This approach lays the foundation for sustainable success, prosperity, and positive impact.

To illustrate with contemporary instances, let us examine some actual actions taken in real life.

ITC Limited

ITC Limited, a conglomerate interested in agriculture, FMCG, and hospitality, has prioritized sustainability in its business operations. The business has been involved in sustainable agriculture practices, such as e-Choupal, a rural digital infrastructure initiative, and its social and farm forestry program, which helps increase green cover and support livelihoods. ITC's focus on sustainability contributes to equitable rural development and environmental conservation.

FabIndia

FabIndia is an Indian retail business renowned for its wide range of traditional clothing and home furnishing products. What sets them apart is their clear commitment to promoting sustainable and handmade products while supporting rural artisans and craftspeople throughout the country. In addition to their traditional offerings, they focus on value creation by consistently evaluating and optimizing their resources. Thanks to their impressive dedication to quality and sustainability, FabIndia has become a go-to destination for those looking for authentic Indian products while supporting local communities.

By integrating these lessons into their approach to business development, businesses can ensure a robust and thriving future. The timeless lesson offered by this parable is a reminder that success is not just about achieving short-term gains but also about a long-term vision that benefits all stakeholders.

8

Compassion in Commerce

"A man was going down from

Jerusalem to Jericho,

when he was attacked by robbers.

They stripped him of his clothes, beat him,

and went away, leaving him half dead.

A priest happened to be going down the same road,

and when he saw the man,

he passed by on the other side.

So too, a Levite, when he came to the place

and saw him, passed by on the other side.

But a Samaritan, as he travelled,

came where the man was; and when he saw him,

he took pity on him.

He went to him and bandaged his wounds,

pouring on oil and wine.

Then he put the man on his donkey,

brought him to an inn, and took care of him.

The next day he took out two denarii

and gave them to the innkeeper.

'Look after him,' he said, 'and when I return,

I will reimburse you for any extra expense

you may have.'"

Parable of the Good Samaritan
Luke 10:30-37

- A Denarii was the usual daily wage of a day laborer.

The parable of the Good Samaritan is an ancient tale that offers valuable insights into the world of business development strategy. Although it may seem unrelated to the business realm at first glance, a closer analysis reveals essential lessons that could help leaders create successful and sustainable businesses.

The story is about a man who was left half-dead and in need of help. The Samaritan, who was passing by, stopped to help the man and cared for him. The Samaritan's empathy, willingness to go above and beyond, and compassionate approach demonstrate how business leaders can apply a similar approach to customer service to drive growth and achieve positive social impact.

The parable teaches us that customers, like the man in need, often seek assistance and support while navigating the marketplace. It highlights the importance of nurturing customer relationships and providing excellent service as the foundation of a sound business development strategy. Businesses can build trust, loyalty, and a positive reputation by putting the customer's needs first. This, in turn, leads to increased customer satisfaction and retention, which is crucial for long-term success.

Businesses prioritizing customer satisfaction and offering exceptional service are likelier to thrive. Adopting an empathetic approach to customer service enables businesses to differentiate themselves from their competition, foster positive social impact, and drive growth. The parable teaches us how a compassionate and empathetic approach to people in need can have a long-lasting effect. It emphasizes the importance of treating customers with compassion, empathy, and integrity and providing excellent service as the cornerstone of a sound business development strategy.

The Good Samaritan parable offers valuable lessons that could be applied to the business world. By prioritizing customer satisfaction and adopting an empathetic approach to customer service, businesses can build trust, loyalty, and a positive reputation, which are critical for long-term success.

The Missed Opportunities

In the parable, a wounded man is ignored by a priest and a Levite, highlighting missed opportunities in the business world. This analogy can be applied to organizations or individuals who fail to assist their customers when they need it most, prioritizing their interests over their needs. Taking an indifferent approach is equivalent to a business that needs to be made aware of the requirements of its customers. It is essential to have a wise outlook and be willing to explore options others may have overlooked to recognize these opportunities. Businesses that provide substandard service or disregard their customers are letting go of valuable prospects for growth and success. By prioritizing profit over customer needs, such organizations weaken the customer's trust and impede business development, eventually leading to a "half-dead" business. Therefore, businesses must prioritize their customers and need to ensure long-term success and growth.

Building Lasting Customer Relationships

The Good Samaritan parable is a well-known story that teaches valuable lessons that can be applied in various aspects of life, including business. The Samaritan's compassionate approach towards the injured man illustrates the importance of empathy, active listening, and concrete actions to help others. This approach is often called a "customer-centric" mindset in the business world. It involves prioritizing customers' needs, concerns, and feedback and taking steps to address them promptly and effectively.

Creating solid and lasting customer relationships requires significant time, effort, and resources. However, the benefits of these relationships include increased customer loyalty, sustainable growth, and a competitive edge. Successful businesses understand that prioritizing the well-being of their customers, employees, and communities is the right thing to do and a sound business strategy.

To establish robust customer relationships, businesses must actively listen to their customers, understand their concerns, and take prompt and effective actions to address them. This involves going beyond the primary customer service requirements and demonstrating empathy, compassion, and a genuine desire to help. By doing so, businesses can create a loyal customer base that returns and advocates for their brand.

Empathy is the cornerstone of building strong customer relationships. It involves treating customers as partners rather than mere sources of revenue. This approach requires businesses to understand their customers' unique needs and preferences and tailor their products, services, and interactions accordingly. By doing so, businesses can create a personalized and memorable customer experience that fosters long-lasting relationships. In summary, committing to robust customer relationships is a matter of ethical responsibility and intelligent business strategy, and it requires a customer-centric mindset that prioritizes empathy, active listening, and prompt action.

Resolving Customer Issues

The story of the Good Samaritan is a powerful reminder of the importance of showing compassion and taking practical measures to resolve problems. In the story, the Samaritan tends to the injured man's wounds and goes above and beyond to meet his needs. He demonstrated a deep understanding of the situation and took action to address the underlying issues.

This same level of understanding and action is crucial in business as well. To truly serve our customers, providing a product or service and tackling their underlying issues and challenges is essential. This requires a commitment to prioritizing the needs of our customers in our strategy.

By prioritizing customers, businesses can identify pain points, unmet needs, and opportunities for improvement. This means providing products or services that meet customer demands, remaining flexible and responsive to customer requests, addressing customer queries, resolving issues immediately, and enhancing the overall customer experience.

The Samaritan's actions teach us that to serve our customers truly, we must be willing to adapt and innovate even in the most challenging situations. Excellent opportunities can emerge when we go beyond traditional boundaries and reach out to our customers. Businesses that are inclusive, adaptable, and willing to engage with diverse customer segments frequently discover untapped markets and experience growth that outpaces their expectations.

Timely communication and problem-solving demonstrate your commitment to customer satisfaction. By addressing concerns and improving weaknesses, you heal your customers' "wounds" and build trust and credibility. Businesses can create long-lasting customer relationships and achieve sustainable success through these actions.

Going the Extra Mile

The parable of the Good Samaritan is a timeless story that teaches us the importance of genuine kindness and compassion. It reminds us that true kindness goes beyond superficial gestures and involves going above and beyond to provide comprehensive support and assistance. This principle is also applicable in business, where businesses that prioritize customer service have the potential to distinguish themselves from their competitors by offering exceptional service that surpasses customer expectations.

To achieve this, businesses must build lasting customer relationships by providing value-added services and unwavering support. This can be achieved by tailoring solutions to meet customer needs, anticipating their needs before they are expressed, and providing personalized support. Businesses prioritizing customer satisfaction over profits are more likely to build a positive corporate image and foster brand loyalty.

Transparency and accountability are also essential components of excellent customer service. Businesses must be transparent in their actions and decisions and take ownership of shortcomings by making amends where necessary. They should also measure their success based on the impact on customers and the communities they serve, not just on profits. Supporting struggling businesses or entrepreneurs, investing in research and development, offering valuable services, or providing necessary resources are all ways in which businesses can contribute to the greater good.

Businesses can create fortified and enduring partnerships, positive reviews, and word-of-mouth marketing by providing exceptional service and demonstrating a commitment to their customers. Ultimately, customers value and appreciate businesses that exceed expectations and offer more than a transactional exchange. So, businesses must build lasting relationships with their customers, provide personalized support, and contribute to the greater good to create a positive and lasting impact.

Sustainable Customer Service

In the parable of the Good Samaritan, the act of a Samaritan paying for the care of a wounded man emphasizes the importance of consistent and reliable customer service. In the corporate world, customer service teams play the role of Samaritans by utilizing data to scrutinize customer interactions, preferences, and needs. By adopting a data-driven approach, businesses can enhance their products, services, and strategies to ensure optimal efficiency and client satisfaction.

Establishing trust is crucial for businesses to maintain customer loyalty. Businesses can achieve this by adopting multi-channel support systems that offer consistent backing across various touchpoints to ensure uninterrupted service. Customer service should be sustainable, address long-term needs, resolve issues promptly, and provide customer satisfaction throughout their journey.

Maintaining customer trust leads to loyalty and repeat business, vital for business growth. Therefore, businesses must continue the noble work initiated by the Samaritan and ensure that the customer's journey is convenient, reliable, and secure. By doing so, they earn their customers' trust and loyalty and ensure their business's long-term success.

Integrity and Long-Term Commitment

The parable of the Good Samaritan teaches us a valuable lesson about building solid and lasting customer relationships. In the business world, this translates to developing a business strategy that prioritizes integrity and a commitment to establishing long-term relationships with customers. Rather than solely focusing on immediate profits, a sustainable business development strategy considers the lifetime value of customers. This involves continual support, follow-up services, and post-purchase engagement to build trust and encourage repeat business. The goal is to create an ongoing value and support system that fosters customer loyalty.

Businesses that consistently provide exceptional customer support and services establish a positive reputation that attracts new customers and strengthens their position in the marketplace. Collaborating with partners and other businesses that align with your mission can increase the value you provide to your customers, build trust, and foster repeat business. Similarly, investing in growth, whether through financial investment, talent development, or social responsibility, while keeping a long-term perspective in mind is essential for a business's success. Honoring promises, taking responsibility, and ensuring customer satisfaction builds trust and loyalty.

Developing a customer-centric strategy is crucial for businesses, and the Good Samaritan approach emphasizes just that. It involves understanding, empathizing, and responding to customers' needs. Like the Good Samaritan's commitment to returning to cover the additional costs incurred, businesses must commit to continuous improvement and innovation to better serve their customers. Every aspect of a business, from product development to marketing to customer care, should revolve around satisfying and delighting customers. However, the parable also reminds us that sometimes unconventional solutions can be the most effective.

Nowadays, there's no better way to make a point than by using real-life examples. With that in mind, let's look at some actions taken in the real world.

Salesforce

Salesforce is a noteworthy customer relationship management (CRM) software business renowned for emphasizing compassionate leadership. The business's CEO, Marc Benioff, is widely recognized for his philanthropic pursuits and commitment to promoting equality and social justice. This approach has helped in the creation of a positive corporate culture, which further enhanced the reputation of the business.

Unilever

Unilever is a globally recognized consumer goods corporation that has established itself as an advocate for ethical business practices. The business strongly emphasizes sustainability and social responsibility, setting ambitious goals to minimize its environmental footprint. By prioritizing ethical practices, Unilever has reinforced its brand reputation and enhanced cost-effectiveness.

In today's fast-paced business landscape, where customer expectations constantly evolve, corporations can benefit from the teachings of the Good Samaritan to achieve success. By emulating the timeless values of compassion, dedication, and integrity that this parable embodies, businesses can cultivate robust customer relations, offer exceptional service, and thrive in the marketplace. The lessons of the Good Samaritan can enable businesses to stay ahead of the competition by remaining attentive to the evolving needs of their customers. Providing superior service and fostering strong customer relations are ethical imperatives and sustainable business strategies that can drive growth and prosperity. Following this example, businesses can establish a legacy of trust, loyalty, and expansion in an increasingly dynamic and interconnected world.

Forging Prosperity

"A king who wanted to settle

accounts with his servants.

As he began the settlement, a man who owed him

ten thousand bags of gold was brought to him.

Since he was not able to pay, the master ordered

that he and his wife and his children

and all that he had to be sold to repay the debt.

"At this, the servant fell on his knees before him.

'Be patient with me,' he begged,

'and I will pay back everything.'

The servant's master took pity on him,

canceled the debt, and let him go.

"But when that servant went out, he found one of his

fellow servants who owed him

a hundred silver coins.

He grabbed him and began to choke him.

'Pay back what you owe me!' he demanded.

"His fellow servant fell to his knees and begged him,

'Be patient with me, and I will pay it back.'

"But he refused. Instead, he went off and

had the man imprisoned until he could pay the debt.

When the other servants saw what had happened,

they were outraged and went and told

their master everything that had happened.

"Then the master called the servant in.

'You wicked servant,' he said,

'I canceled all that debt of yours

because you begged me to.

Shouldn't you have had mercy

on your fellow servant just as I had on you?'

In anger, his master handed him over to the jailers

to be tortured, until he should pay back all he owed."

Parable of Unmerciful Servant
Mathew 18:23-34

The parable, "The king who wanted to settle accounts with his servants," is a timeless and thought-provoking narrative with significant implications for business development. Its underlying message emphasizes mercy, compassion, and understanding in our dealings with others, particularly in financial transactions and relationships. The story revolves around a king who seeks transparency and accountability from his servants, who owe him significant money. This scenario is commonplace in business, where leaders and stakeholders evaluate financial matters and organizational relationships.

The parable's central narrative creates a compelling backdrop for unfolding events, providing crucial insights into the dynamics of ethical leadership, forgiveness, empathy, and reciprocity. The king's desire for clarity and accountability encourages his servants to come forth and reveal their debts. One of them owes a vast sum he cannot repay, and the king orders him and his family to be sold to settle the debt. The servant pleads for mercy, and the king, moved by compassion, forgives the debt entirely.

The parable's lessons are profound and applicable to various aspects of business development. The king's actions demonstrate the importance of empathy and forgiveness, even when harsh punishment seems justified. The servant's behavior warns against greed, dishonesty, and a lack of compassion, which can have dire consequences for individuals and organizations. The parable's message also highlights the significance of ethical leadership, transparency, and accountability in fostering growth, success, and sustainable business relationships.

Overall, the parable of "The king who wanted to settle accounts with his servants" is a powerful allegory that provides valuable insights for entrepreneurs, executives, and professionals seeking to comprehend the dynamics of ethical leadership, empathy, and sustainable business growth. Its timeless account of debt forgiveness and the consequences of a lack of compassion is a persuasive and inspiring parable that can help individuals and organizations build strong and meaningful relationships.

Debt Forgiveness as an Investment and Business Opportunities

In the story, a king begins by calling his servants to settle their accounts, highlighting the importance of financial accountability and responsibility. This emphasizes the crucial aspect of business development, where financial matters hold significant value. The protagonist, a man who owes an enormous debt to the king, is a metaphor for entrepreneurs, startups, or businesses burdened with financial obligations. In business, debt can take multiple forms, such as loans, investments, or outstanding payments, and managing them responsibly is a vital aspect of business development.

The king's decision to address these debts demonstrates the importance of promptly taking care of financial matters to maintain a healthy economic ecosystem. The story's defining moment comes when the servant, who has an insurmountable debt, pleads for mercy. The king, exhibiting empathy and compassion, forgives him of his entire debt, demonstrating the concept of "forgiveness as an investment." The master's decision to dismiss the whole debt is an unexpected act of mercy. This act of forgiving the debt can be compared to the business practice of understanding the needs and challenges of others in the business world. In the business world, this concept can be likened to debt restructuring, where creditors forgive part of a business's debt in exchange for a better long-term business relationship. It illustrates the importance of helping, especially when a business partner or employee is in trouble.

Moreover, businesses can benefit by showing compassion and giving a second chance to suppliers, employees, partners, or customers who have made mistakes or fallen short of expectations. The servant's request for patience and promise to repay his debt illustrates the art of negotiation. Negotiating favorable terms, exercising forbearance, and offering second chances can foster loyalty and trust, leading to more enduring relationships and long-term partnerships, ultimately benefiting the business's development.

The king's cancellation of debts can be seen as a metaphor for opening new business opportunities through a fresh start. The story encourages business owners to prioritize financial responsibility, debt management, and compassion, emphasizing that these practices can foster positive relationships and benefit the long-term development of their businesses. In conclusion, the story highlights the importance of financial accountability, debt management, and compassion in business, which can ultimately lead to a prosperous business venture.

Ethical Leadership and Compassion

Forgiveness is a crucial ethical leadership trait that can significantly impact an organization's success and growth. It is a quality that promotes compassion, empathy, and fairness, vital attributes for leaders. Leaders who demonstrate forgiveness set a positive example of ethical behavior and hold individuals accountable for their actions, which can lead to a culture of empathy, forgiveness, and integrity. This culture can drive sustainable growth and success in an organization.

Empathy is another essential attribute for entrepreneurs and leaders in the business world. Leaders who demonstrate empathy and compassion towards their employees, customers, and partners can establish productive, long-lasting relationships. By understanding the needs and challenges of their stakeholders, leaders can create a positive work environment that fosters creativity, innovation, and sustainable growth. Employees who feel engaged and satisfied are more likely to contribute to the business's development and success, leading to greater profitability and competitive advantage.

The story of the king's act of forgiveness highlights the critical role of leadership in shaping an organization's culture. Leaders who lead by example and encourage ethical behavior, compassion, and forgiveness in their teams can promote a culture that values empathy, fairness, and integrity. This culture can drive sustainable growth and success in an organization and attract top talent and loyal customers. In summary, forgiveness and empathy are essential traits for leaders in today's business world, and they can significantly impact an organization's success and growth.

Shortcomings of Vengeance

The parable's pivotal moment exposes the darker aspects of human nature, wherein the forgiven servant exhibits no mercy towards another servant who owes him a comparatively small amount. This type of conduct is frequently mirrored in business settings where individuals refuse to pardon minor debts or errors, causing strained relationships and unproductive disputes.

The story highlights the importance of empathy and forgiveness in business relationships. The forgiven servant's lack of empathy in dealing with his colleague's debts exemplifies an unproductive approach to business. His harsh actions result in a backlash from the afflicted servant and his colleagues, who are appalled by his behavior.

The parable is a cautionary tale for business leaders who may be tempted to hold grudges or seek revenge against their colleagues. Instead of demonstrating the same compassion he received, the forgiven servant resorts to violence and is subsequently imprisoned. This is a stark reminder that resentment and the desire for revenge can harm business development.

In business, the keys to growth are collaboration, trust, and a willingness to resolve disputes amicably. By putting oneself in the shoes of others and understanding their challenges, businesses can cultivate an atmosphere of comprehension and mutual support conducive to development and growth. Treating others with kindness and forgiveness can lead to positive outcomes in business relationships and foster a culture of respect and cooperation.

Reputation and Public Opinion

The parable is a cautionary tale that warns against the dangers of hypocrisy and a lack of reciprocity. It tells of a servant who owed a large debt and was forgiven by his master. The servant demonstrated remarkable kindness by seeking forgiveness, and his master showed mercy and compassion by forgiving the debt. However, when the same servant encountered another who owed him a much smaller debt, he failed to extend the same kindness and forgiveness he had received. This behavior highlights the risks of lacking empathy, understanding, and sound business conduct in the corporate world.

The parable serves as a reminder that more than receiving help is needed in business. One must also offer support and understanding to others facing challenges. The forgiven servant's actions demonstrate the negative impact that a lack of compassion and knowledge can have. His behavior left a poor impression of his character and the opinion of others. Fellow servants witnessed his lack of empathy and reported the incident to their master. This underscores the importance of reputation management in business development.

When businesses set unreasonable standards for their partners, it can lead to strained relationships and hinder cooperation. A reputation for impartiality, compassion, and integrity can go a long way in establishing trust and building successful business relationships. Customers and partners are likelier to work with, invest in, or recommend a business known for its ethical behavior and fair dealings, ultimately contributing to sustainable development.

Therefore, ethical behavior must be a top priority for businesses. Building a reputation for impartiality, honesty, and integrity can establish trust, a cornerstone for successful business relationships. The parable is a timeless reminder that empathy, compassion, and ethical business conduct are essential for personal growth and a business's growth and success.

Consequences of Unethical Business Practices

The parable of the Unforgiving Servant is a powerful story that warns us about the dire consequences of engaging in unethical business practices. In this parable, the king denounces the unforgiving servant for his lack of compassion and subjects him to punishment until he repays his debt.

We can draw parallels between this story and the world of business, where businesses that fall short of prioritizing empathy and mutual support face various consequences. These consequences can include a negative impact on their reputation, strained partnerships, and reduced opportunities for growth. Just as the unforgiving servant's unethical conduct towards his colleague cast aspersions on his reputation and led to adverse effects, businesses that resort to exploitative tactics risk facing legal, financial, and reputational repercussions that can impede growth.

To ensure sustainable prosperity and success, businesses must adhere to ethical standards. This means prioritizing empathy and mutual support, treating colleagues and partners somewhat, and avoiding unethical practices. By doing so, businesses can build a strong reputation, earn the trust of their partners, and create opportunities for growth and success. The parable of the unforgiving servant serves as a powerful warning and a reminder of the importance of ethical behavior in business.

Learning from Mistakes

The parable presented in the text is a powerful reminder of the importance of learning from one's mistakes and taking responsibility for one's actions, especially in business development. Recognizing and rectifying errors is essential for progress and success in any organization. Businesses that embrace this principle often enjoy positive outcomes, including a strong reputation, fruitful partnerships, and a loyal customer base.

Rather than being viewed as failures, mistakes can be seen as opportunities for improvement and development. A culture of learning, combined with a commitment to continuous progress, can pave the way for success. Drawing parallels between this timeless story and the modern business world can provide insight into fostering a harmonious, growth-oriented, and ethical environment within businesses. By doing so, businesses can strive for financial success while also having a positive impact on their employees, partners, and the community at large.

Consider the following real-life actions as present-day examples.

Mahindra & Mahindra

Mahindra & Mahindra, an automotive and multinational corporation, has demonstrated the importance of ethical leadership and transparency in the corporate world. The business's leaders, such as Anand Mahindra, have emphasized sustainability, social responsibility, and ethical business practices. The business has fostered strong relationships with customers, employees, and partners by adhering to these principles, contributing to its long-term success.

Wipro

Wipro, another primary IT services business in India, strongly emphasizes ethical leadership and corporate responsibility. The business's leaders, including Azim Premji, have been vocal proponents of ethical business conduct and sustainability. Wipro's commitment to responsible business practices includes transparency in its dealings, ethical sourcing, and accountability to shareholders and the broader community. This approach has helped Wipro build solid and lasting relationships with clients and stakeholders.

Moreover, the parable emphasizes the importance of financial responsibility, the power of empathy and compassion, and the need for reciprocity in building solid and lasting business relationships. Entrepreneurs, leaders, and professionals who consider these lessons can build more substantial, sustainable businesses that achieve financial success and positively impact their reputation and social environment.

Therefore, it is essential to understand the significance of these principles and apply them to business practices. By doing so, businesses can create an ethical and sustainable environment that promotes growth and prosperity. This, in turn, can positively impact the community, creating a win-win situation for all stakeholders involved. In sum, the parables presented in the book offer valuable insights into the fundamental principles of success and sustainability in business development.

"Every work is a business,

and every businessperson is a dedicated worker,

for in the labor of ambition, the sweat of innovation,

and the persistence of purpose,

they forge the **FUTURE**.*"*

Samson Samuel